THE SCENT of ANGELS

Battlefield Memories

by

Margaret Le Grange

All rights reserved. No part of this publication may be reproduced, converted or archived into any other medium without a relevant permission first being obtained from the publisher. Nor should the book be circulated or resold in any binding other than its original cover.

The Scent of Angels: Battlefield Memories

© Margaret Le Grange 1996

First Edition published February 2005

Cover artwork by Jean Hands

Photograph reproduced by permission of Jean Hands

Printed & Published by:
St Ives Printing & Publishing Company,
High Street, St Ives, Cornwall TR26 1RS, UK.

ISBN 0 948385 37 5

THE SCENT *of* ANGELS
Battlefield Memories

Foreword
Chapter 1   'Passchendael' – George's story (Groobie Alteringham)
Chapter 2   'In Flanders Fields' – John's story (Jack)
Chapter 3   'Unknown Soldier' – Jock McCree's story
Chapter 4   'Shot as a Coward' – William's story (Willy)
Chapter 5   'Behind the Lines' – Frank's story
Chapter 6   'Flanders – The King's Shilling' – Samuel's story (1)
Chapter 7   'On a Wing and a Prayer' – Tom's story
Chapter 8   'Rodney's Story'
Chapter 9   'Mayday, Mayday' – Teddy's story
Chapter 10 'Tobruk' – Johnny's story
Chapter 11 'Fjords' – Andersen's story
Chapter 12 'Kuala Lumpur' – Kristine's story
Chapter 13 'Auschwitz' – Samuel's story (2)
Chapter 14 'Hurricane' – Timothy's story
Chapter 15 'Dunkirk' – Andrew's story
Chapter 16 'Sweet Smell of Death' – David's story
Chapter 17 'Burma Railway' – Lawrence and Edmond's story
Chapter 18 'Yvette – Mademoiselle de la Nuit' – Yvette's story
Chapter 19 'Andy, Morris and Claud's Story'
Chapter 20 'Farewell Kiss' – Malcolm's story
Chapter 21 'Dresden' – Ginger's story
Chapter 22 'I Was There' – Michael's story
Chapter 23 'One of Our Planes is Missing' – Matthew's story
Chapter 24 'Blown to Bits' – Josh's story

Chapter 25   'The Battle of Midway' – Simon's story
Chapter 26   'The Last Jump' – James' story

Any communication for claiming a relative please contact:
    Margaret Le Grange
    Guide Light Cottage
    38 Boscaswell Village
    Pendeen; Cornwall; TR19 7EP

FOREWORD

I was born in Salisbury, Southern Rhodesia in 1937, my father was born in Edinburgh, and my mother came from Lancashire, they were out there for twenty-one years, farming and growing tobacco. I was the second child of four.

As a family who moved around a lot, I ended up going to thirteen schools. The last being in the UK after we came home after the war, was a Rudolf Steiner school, one of the first ones of its kind then in the UK. It was in my final year at school I started to hear things and knew when things were going to happen, but I did not then understand what was happening to me.

In the 1990's I finally became a Spiritualist which lead on to things as they are now. I write in long hand, and in pencil, this way I don't get cramp, also I am in Semi trance and the writing is called Automatic writing.

Finally after writing in the *Battlefield Memories,* which has taken ten years to complete, I am getting them published. Have to do it privately as no publisher understands this work, strange as it might seem, most have published Psychic books before.

I hope with the publication of this book, I will be able to find a few more families who can claim their relative, this is the reason I have been chosen by spirit to be a scribe for SOUL RESCUE.

All the stories are true, and have been cross referenced where possible, this shows you that there is LIFE after DEATH.

I have been psychic since childhood, but did not know which path I was meant to take until 1993. It started in May of that year, when my father made contact with me. We were always close on earth, so it didn't seem strange to start talking to him again.

At first I sat and we would chat, whilst I wrote it all down. I had been told by a medium two years previously that I would have my chosen path given to me by my father, and that Spirit wanted me to be a scribe for them. My father said to me 'You don't have to watch the clock, as there is no time in the spirit world. I will put the words to write into your mind. I speak for you − I am your thoughts.' He also said 'Knowledge from the spirit world is a priceless gem to be treasured.'

In 1993, before starting to write, I trained to become a Spiritual Healer, following in my father's footsteps.

For three years I wrote, talking to my father, writing philosophy before starting on my war stories. 1996 I first wrote three booklets of psychic poems and was then fully in harness as a channel and 'Rainbow Bridge' for the spirit world. The title that my work was to be written under, *The Scent of Angels*, was given to me in a dream.

Young soldiers came to stand beside me, always on my right side, and told me of their last moments of life on earth. All had been posted 'Missing, presumed dead.' I cross-reference their information as much as I can. My father had said 'I want you to get this information published.' After an illness and a gap of seven months without writing, I had a stroke, I longed to write again. When one is ill Spirit always steps back, as one can't work if not 100% fit.

I asked one morning whether they thought I was ready to start again. I sat down and was immediately in contact with Spirit once more, writing Fairy Stories.

Margaret Le Grange

A SONNET for ANNIE

I walk through the portals of time
And step back from my bright world to thine.
The love that held me so long ago
Calls me back once more.
What makes you grieve so?
Let go of your earthly ties
And come to me once more.
Let us be reunited Soul to Soul again.
Here, hold my hand, I come for you.
Nothing to fear my loved one, my darling.
Time has come for you to come home,
Those War years so long ago
Tore us apart. You grieved so,
Now your raven hair is white as snow,
Tears like pearls,
Your eyes are deep crystal pools.
You never married. You could have done so
But our love was strong enough
To last for eternity.
I have never been far away all those years.
Come, my darling, come fly through the Heavenly
Portals of time and light; come home to me,
I've waited so long for you − I never grew old.
Soon you will be young again and free from pain.
Your spirit will fly free, dance and sing once more.
Here, take my hand, I come for thee.
I loved you, and we will love once more.
My waiting time is ended.

Passchendaele

I walk through the Portals of Time.

I was barely seventeen when the War took me away from Annie, my sweetheart, and we vowed that we would get married when the War ended; but for me it ended sooner than I had expected. I used to write sonnets for Annie – now we will soon be together again.

For me, those years have meant little in time as I have been in a most fascinating world of light and love, but I have never forgotten my wee lass, my lovely Annie. I've watched over her and loved her from my world, and have even been beside her, touched her face, kissed her lips, but she never knew.

I wish she had known that I never left her. I promised, as sweethearts do 'I will love you till I die'. I didn't know then that love never dies, and that I could come back to your world at a thought, travel through time and space with no effort, no barriers and no front lines.

In the War there was the sound of gunfire, the smell of poisonous mustard gas, mud, flies and the fear – yes, the utter fear of death. We could smell death, taste it, see it; when would it be my time? I often prayed 'Lord, please spare me all this hell.'

Hell it was at Passchendaele in 1917. One by one my comrades fell – one moment I was talking to Danny and the next moment he had gone, blown away by shell blast, face down in the mud.

We drowned in mud, it never stopped raining and we were chilled to the bone. I got it with a mustard attack – oh God, I couldn't get my mask on in time and the Army didn't know that the masks were of little use. Mustard gas burnt our skin, blinded our eyes and destroyed our lungs. The memories of those horrendous days in those Hellhole trenches caused it to be a long time before I could smell the Heavenly flowers.

Danny was my best mate – perhaps he will come through to you. It's easier than I thought, but then I didn't know that I could talk to anyone and be heard. I tried to talk to Annie, but she never heard me. In a short time from now, Annie and I will be reunited – I love her so.

Danny and I were killed on the same day. I don't think I could have lasted another day without my buddy; we were like brothers and grew up together as farmers' lads in the same village in Suffolk. I passed over on November 10th. 1917 – I was only seventeen. My name was George, nicknamed Groobie.

God bless you and thank you. Now I know I can talk to Annie as we will be together by nightfall of this day, November 15th. 1997.

George was 5'8" approximately, of slim build with brown hair and eyes. He had a long nose, a lovely wide grin and always chewed on a straw. When I asked George his surname I got something like Alteringham and Annie Brownshaw.

IN FLANDERS FIELDS

'In Flanders fields where poppies grow . . .' is the first line of a famous 1st. World War poem. I shed my blood on Flanders fields, along with hundreds of my comrades. It was our blood that made the barren fields fertile, and as the poppies grew they symbolised our blood in the redness of their colours.

I was fighting on the front line in 1915, but wasn't out there very long. My death was horrific, but most early, violent death is horrific. I was killed by a shell blast and landed on the barbed wire − no one came to take me down, so I think they thought that I had been killed outright.

I remember standing beside this body of mine, torn to pieces, wondering what I was doing there. This couldn't be me, could it? I felt no more pain and didn't know that no one could see me. I looked at my new radiant body − no bullet holes, no blood. What was I doing here? Where was I going?

Gradually, during the passing hours, I was joined by more and more comrades and some were even Germans. We formed small groups as the battle raged. There was no hate in our hearts for the Germans, who were as young as I was − we all felt compassion for each other. Guns, cannons and bombs went raging on around us but we were untouched. At that moment in time I didn't really know that I was dead. How could I? I could see and hear noises around me, which the others could also see.

Then all went quiet, not because the fighting had ceased, but because we started to float above the ground and then far above the battlefield, gaining speed. I was pulled up towards the light, faster and faster. I could hear sweet music, smell flowers and beautiful things appeared in my sight. This was such a contrast to what I had witnessed and heard a few moments before. I was being pulled further and further, faster and faster, then all was peaceful.

We had all feared the thought of dying and I was so scared as I didn't know what to expect. No one ever told me it would be like this. If we had known before we went into battle, we would have had something to look forward to when our time on earth came to an end.

My name was John, known as Jack to all my family. When I lived on earth, I lived in Crawley in Sussex. I loved Sussex, the rolling valleys, neat hedges and wooded hillsides. I worked on the land as a hedger and ditcher, and was a craftsman like my Pa and Grandpa. Working with billhooks, we could cut the hedges in layers and bend them into a tight, living hedge.

It's ironic, if you think about it, that I died on a barbed wire fence – a cruel twist of fate. I was just eighteen when I left the fields of Flanders and passed in January 1915. As I said, I died and found myself standing beside my body, not able to do anything but not wanting to leave it alone in a blood soaked foreign land.

Thank you for hearing me and taking down my story. I'm OK now, but it took me a long time to come to terms with my death.

Received on February 7th. 1999. Jack was claimed as Ann Harrington's grandfather. She lives in Boscaswell, Pendeen but comes from the London area.

UNKNOWN SOLDIER
Buried at Westminster Abbey

My name was Jock McCree and I was in the Black Watch Regiment in Flanders. During a heavy bombardment I was hit by shrapnel – in fact, my body was peppered with it. We were all getting ready to go over the top when the shell blast hit our trench. We had no idea that we were so close to the enemy lines, though sometimes we could smell them. The smell of their cooking and their dead came drifting across in the autumn mists. The smell of death is not nice. I often wondered if they could smell us.

Unlike so many of my comrades, when I fell I was given an honourable funeral and a grave stone. I'm sure that I did not deserve such an honour. I would have liked my final resting-place to have been in Scotland, the land of my birth. When they called me The Unknown Soldier, I was not in fact unknown as I was wearing my regimental uniform and dog tags, but there were so many of us that day who died under shell blast, blown to pieces. I felt that soldiers who had been out in Flanders much longer than me deserved this great honour more. However, when it came to it, I had no choice.

Now, what I want to say to you, my lassie, is that for eighty years I have tried to reach out from my world at this special time, to let someone know it was me. Today I saw a white light shining out of the darkness during that two minutes silence and your thoughts caught my attention. Your thoughts were 'Anyone out there who wants to use my Rainbow Bridge come and talk to me – tell me your story. I will be waiting for you to come.'

When I made contact, I saw you write down my name, Jock McCree, so at last I have made contact. What amazes me is that you can hear my thoughts as I heard yours, and then you write them down. That's what is so amazing.

I was born in Edinburgh in the year 1889 and was just twenty-five years old when I died. I joined as a regular soldier and died in 1914 – I loved the life, never thinking at the time that I would be fighting in a war in a far away land. I remember, about twenty five years ago, a song sung in Scotland called *A Scottish Soldier* – that could have been me. It might surprise you that I was often at home with my parents afterwards, trying to let them know what had happened to me, but they never knew I was there. We were not a well off family – many a meal at home was porridge and broth – but that's what made us men.

I must admit, I did swagger 'aboot' a bit and fancied myself wearing the kilt and all the gear – a good catch for the lassies, but I didn't get round to settling down with a wife and bairn. I wish I had now, knowing what life held in store for me. Lost opportunities are a great regret. Well, I bid you farewell and God bless and thank you for the white light of welcome.

Jock was thickset, about 5'8" tall with a shock of red/auburn hair and green eyes. He had a ruddy complexion and liked his dram of whisky. Received November 14th. 2000.

SHOT as a COWARD

It was March 1916, in Belgium, and it had been raining for endless days. The mud stank and the coldness of my sodden boots was chilling me to the bone. I was an orderly with the Medical Corps. My uniform was khaki and I wore a patch on my shoulder with a red cross on a white background, which was the only marking I wore to make me stand out from the others.

My job was to run along the trenches or 'over the top' in the lulls between fighting, to rescue the living wounded and take them back to the hospital area. This was dangerous work, as one could get caught in crossfire. My name was William (Willy) and my best buddy was Baxter. On this occasion, when we were sent out to look for the wounded, we could hear shouts of 'Stretcher bearers, over here, hurry man.' We had to leave the dead, as there was no helping those poor blighters by then. Between us we carried a stretcher to carry the wounded back, always running half bent over so that our heads didn't show above the top of the trenches, which were quite low in places.

Baxter and I had found a small pocket of badly wounded men. It was on our third run that the firing started up again, and we got caught in the crossfire. Baxter was hit really badly – there was blood everywhere and I couldn't stop the bleeding. I crouched down beside him, cradling his head in my lap. He whimpered like a wounded animal for what seemed a long, long time. Near me was a Chaplain who had been giving the Last Rites to the dying. Then Baxter was gone and I was alone amongst the dead, apart from the Chaplain. We sat and had a smoke, couldn't think of God, couldn't pray and I was unashamedly sobbing. I was covered in mud and soaked with Baxter's blood – my pal had died. The firing went on for hours.

When the noise stopped and the Chaplain got to his feet, he gave me a helping hand to get up. I automatically rolled Baxter on to the stretcher to take him back with me, but the Chaplain said 'Leave him, we must go.' I didn't want to go and leave him. Fear and a cold sweat ran over me and my tears blinded me – I was only seventeen. Baxter was a couple of years older than me and had always told me what to do, so I just couldn't think for myself now. As I stumbled along the trench, over the dead bodies of my comrades, it was so quiet and a damp mist hung like a shroud over the ground, as it was now dark.

I had no idea what time it was or how long we had been away. It felt as though the world had stopped living and time had stood still. We seemed to be going the wrong way as I had lost my bearings and couldn't remember which way I had originally gone – everything looked the same. Then one of our men shot the Chaplain by mistake, thinking that he was a German who had infiltrated our lines. I managed to shout 'Blimey, mate, it's me – Willy, the doc's orderly.' I did not know the password.

All hell broke out with the shouting, and then the Major appeared. He said 'Arrest that man' and I said 'Who me?' 'Yes, arrest him as a coward'. It seems that I had been missing for twelve hours and they said I had deserted my post.

I had no one to talk to, or to speak up for me, as the Chaplain was dead. All hope died in the next few minutes as I was handcuffed and marched off between two soldiers. I wasn't given a chance to explain how we had been cut off from the rest, and I had stayed with the Chaplain who was now dead, killed by one of our own men. We had been cut off by crossfire and I had stayed with Baxter, who had died on my lap – hence the blood. They just wouldn't listen to me.

There was another young soldier with me. He had tried to run away and had been caught, so we were to be made an example of for any men who might have had ideas of being cowardly and running away. The next morning, at daybreak, I was marched out, tied to a post, blindfolded and shot – by our own men. At least the war was over for me then. I just want you to know that I wasn't a coward. Maybe, if I had had a gun and fired it, that might have helped in my defence, but I was a stretcher-bearer and couldn't fire when my hands were full.

My Ma and Pa had to live with the shame of being told that I was a coward. Someone even sent them a white feather, to indicate that their only son had let his country down. This is why I came today, to tell my own story. My parents had to live with the stigma of disgrace for the rest of their lives, but I knew that if there was a God anywhere, in the eyes of God I was innocent of cowardice.

Thank you for writing down my story. Willy.

Willy was a slim lad with thin black hair and brown eyes. He looked young for his age. Received in June 1998.

BEHIND the LINES

Hello, I'm Frank. I started my life, from a week old, in an orphanage in Wales. I was taken from my mother, as I was born out of wedlock when she was sixteen years old. Life in the orphanage was harsh, with frequent beatings for no apparent reason. The place was cold and dark, with bars at the windows – like a prison with small children as inmates. The odd photograph was taken for the benefit of the Parish. My mother's friend worked there as a cook and so was able to keep her in touch with the progress of her little son.

At eight years old I was sent down the mine, and being small and rather frail was given the job of looking after the pit ponies. Most of the ponies were blind, having worked underground all their lives. When I was fourteen the First World War broke out, and the older boys were the first to join up and get the King's Shilling. I joined when I was just sixteen, as it was said that they needed more fighting men at the Front. We were told that the war would not last long, but it dragged on for years.

As I had experience with horses, I was given the job of feeding, grooming and harnessing the horses ready to go into battle. Many of them had been made deaf by gunfire. I had thought that life was cruel enough for the pit ponies, but this was barbaric. The noble beasts were sent to their slaughter, pulling the gun carriages to the Front Line – their wounds were terrible to see, and their screams haunted us.

We had a veterinarian on duty who was kind to the horses. He would remove bullets and stitch them up, only to see them being sent out again when fit. Like men, they suffered from shell shock and shook all the time. When this was really bad, or they had broken legs, they were shot and the butchered meat given to the men to eat. I never fancied eating my friends.

On that occasion, Winston and I had to take the cannon up to the lines, but were caught in crossfire. We toppled into a shell hole with the cannon – a really tangled mess – then a shell blast hit us. Winston was the troops' mascot and had served his masters well. He died first, and then me, and we lay together side by side. Like so many thousands, I was never found.

We never knew what lay ahead of us, and it was such a pity that these beautiful animals also had to die in that way. I was sixteen when I died in that shell hole in Flanders in 1916, having been out there only a short while.

When my mother lay dying, I came for her and we are now together. We all try to forget the past and how we died, but events on the earth plane arise to bring the old memories flooding back.

Thank you for writing down my story.

Received on 29th. June 2002.

FLANDERS – THE KING'S SHILLING

Hello, my name is Samuel. I worked on the land as my Da was a gamekeeper for a big country house in Dorset. I learned my trade as a hedger and ditcher.

I loved the life – those early autumn days with the thick haw frost shining like gems in the trees and lying like a crystal carpet on the fields. The hoarse cry of a cock pheasant and the bark of a fox made those the happiest days of my life.

I was seventeen when I took the King's Shilling and found myself out on the fields of Flanders, lying in trenches of stinking, icy mud. Oh God, how cold we were – our clothes never dried out and our feet would rot in our boots, but then, if you lived longer than a week you were lucky. The deprivation, humiliation, starvation, disease and our low morale made us a pitiful sight. Hand to hand combat meant fix bayonets, climb out of the trench and go over the top.

We would write our letters home, those of us who could write, and tuck them inside our uniforms to keep them dry. Some of us never did get them collected to be sent home.

In those cold, wet hours of waiting for the whistle to blow, I would dream once again of those autumns in Dorset – the lovely smell of damp earth and bonfires, the stillness of the dawns and the nights bright with stars. I was a simple lad and loved my life on the land, finding so much pleasure in everything I saw.

Now, what a contrast, no sun or moon, only mud, flies and the stench of blood and the dead. There was no time to bury our comrades, no time to live again.

I was shot in my third week out in Flanders, on a November day with thick fog. The Germans were on top of us before we knew it. I have been over here a long time. It's lovely here, no more killing or dying, only a lot of love and healing.

I came to you today as this is the anniversary of my passing from the hellhole of Flanders to Heaven. I was coming up to my eighteenth birthday, on November 5th. 1917. My Da called me Sam but my Ma called me Samuel.

God bless and good night. Thank you for letting me come through during your healing circle. I've waited a long time to tell someone my story. Thanks.

Samuel was 6' tall, thin but strong with brown hair and green eyes. He was a simple farm lad, very gentle – unable to read or write.

Cross reference: YPRES (Ee-pruh) or 'Wipers.' Three battles of World War 1 were fought near this town in western Belgium, the first in 1914, the second in 1915 (with poison gas) and the third in 1917, known as Passchendaele. About 300,000 British soldiers died and as many Germans.

5.11.1996. About a week after receiving this, a grave of British soldiers was discovered on a building site. I feel that Samuel's presence now was a timely event. As the soldiers died, they were buried in mass graves, if they were found. After the war they were reburied in military graveyards all over France and Belgium. Samuel's final resting-place only happened last year and some have never been found to this day.

The first time it started I was out on the moors. I heard the engine of a heavy plane, but only saw a smaller one doing figure-of-eight's – then it was gone. I heard these words:

ON a WING and a PRAYER

It was 1941 and my name was Tom.

As the sun began to rise, with the darkened clouds of night still across the skies, we would stand shoulder to shoulder, all in the same stance, hands shading our eyes and ears open to the slightest sounds.

First one would call 'I can hear them coming. I wonder if Joe, Sandy, Ginger or Curly has made it back?' Then, still searching the skies, a tiny speck would come into sight. There was a cough and splutter of an engine and we would hold our breath. Last night our boys had done a good job, but had taken a beating – we lost seven last night, our comrades gone – and we had our sortie tonight.

One, two, three – here they came. Ambulances raced out across the airfield. I know God had a hand in bringing them home and to a safe landing. The crews were tired and red eyed – yes, Sandy was there, and Curly and Joe. 'Thank god' we would silently pray, 'for bringing our brave lads home today.'

As I was saying, it was our turn for a sortie that night. We flew away from the setting sun, aware of the intense colour and heat through our cockpits. I flew a four-engine bomber with a gun turret under its belly. Higher and higher we flew. I had a crew of seven – gunners, navigator, co-pilot, myself and two others – though sometimes we fly short handed. We all silently prayed to God 'Please give us your protection and guide us away from the ack-ack guns (anti aircraft) below. Let us find our target and get home again safely.'

Then we were up in the clouds, pointing over the Channel and leaving England behind. We felt very close to God, as though if we reached out our hands we could hold His hand. We all felt that our lives hung in the balance on the scales of life or death, and God had the power to decide if we would get home in the dawn.

As we approached French soil our eyes scanned the skies for enemy aircraft, who used to hide in the clouds, follow us above or below, playing cat and mouse with us and attacking us when we least expected it. The plane I flew was a heavy thing, and with a full load of bombs we could not afford to be fired on from beneath or we would blow up.

If anyone ever said that they were not afraid, they were liars – we were all terrified, our nerves taut and our eyes strained, unblinking. My crew were young , like me – we would chatter and tell jokes to keep our morale high, but soon fell silent as we droned on. The noise of our plane was so loud that it was hard to hear the whine of the Messerschmitts as they climbed out of the clouds, banked, turned and looped the loop. One moment they would be flying beside us and the next moment they were underneath.

I always thought that our gunner was the pluckiest of all, as he sat like a sitting duck under the belly of our plane. We lost more gunners than anyone else during those early days of the war. There wasn't one of us who really liked what we were doing, but after our tenth mission we became robots, doing everything in a dream. It was a case of either shoot or be shot. On our mission sorties we were flanked by our watchdogs, the spitfires, and we relied on them for our protection, especially over the sea.

My target tonight was an ammunition factory. The night was dark as we got closer to our target, fires burned and the dreaded search lights spread their long fingers into the night, as if reaching up to catch us and pull us down. Stray bullets and flak whizzed by and sometimes we would feel a thump when the odd bullet hit us or tore through our wings. We flew on, almost holding our breath, hoping that we would be able to unload our bombs and, looking back see that we had hit our target – a giant firework display lighting up the sky.

It was on clear nights we could more easily be seen, so we preferred foggy nights or heavy rain. The Huns were often less alert on those nights.

This night we got a bad hit – an engine on the port side was smoking and I had to climb in height hoping to put out the fire which was starting to make itself seen. We had four engines and this was the furthest out on the wing. With a splutter it died on me and the plane shook as the other three engines took over. We had to hold our altitude as our target was dead ahead of us now. All we had to do was fly another mile, drop our bombs and turn for home.

Things started to go wrong, just little things at first. I could not contact the gunner and presumed he had been hit, as all I got was a crackle over the wireless. Our navigator had a small head wound, where a piece of flak had grazed him, coming through the plane. He was dazed but still trying to do his job.

Suddenly, there it was straight ahead. To open the bomb doors we had to pump them manually, then count 'One, two, three – over target – bombs away.' As each bomb was released the plane felt lighter.

I didn't wait to see if we had hit the target, though I knew I should have done, as my main thought was to get home.

It seemed so long before we spotted the Channel shining in the moonlight, with a runway of light leading us home. We must make it back home, but even if I didn't reach our airfield and base, I could bring her down on English soil. Half way across our second engine died, leaving only two on the starboard side. The plane was juddering and it took all my strength to hold her on course – we were limping home. We were also losing altitude, but now at least we were over the Channel and heading for home.

I knew that, with the dawn, our buddies would be standing shoulder to shoulder, waiting for our return. There had been three of us last night, taking off at 19.00 hours and it was now 5.30 am. The outline of Old Blighty was just visible – would we have enough altitude to clear the cliffs? We were so close to the cornfields that I felt I could almost touch the red poppies that swayed in the down draught of the plane. I was sure that we would not get home to base and warned my crew to brace for the crash landing I was prepared to make.

Our gunner was dead, his gun turret blown away. I had lost him somewhere over Germany and prayed to God 'I hope he didn't suffer. Oh God, Almighty pilot of the skies, please guide us home to our loved ones, on a wing and a prayer.'

We did get home that time, and I made six more sorties later – then one time I never did come home. I was buried (what was found of me) in the soil of France, when my luck ran out. But I am not dead. I am alive and here now with you. The memories of the battles I fought and finally lost are now forgotten. I often wonder if others talked to God like we did, and held God's hand in theirs when their final time on earth came.

I don't think my parents ever knew how or where I ended my days, but they do now as we are all together here. I passed from earth in August 1942 – I was just twenty-three. I have not grown old – I am still in my prime.

Thank you for allowing me to communicate through you, and tell my story on the anniversary of my passing.

God bless you. May I come again?

I am your pilot, to guide you on your life's path.

Tom was 6', with ginger hair and grey/green twinkling eyes. He was a sportsman with a clean young face, who liked to dress smartly. 7th August 1996

Cross reference taken from An Illustrated History of the RAF *by Roy Conyers Nesbit. Four engine bombers with gun turrets under the belly, used by 90 Squadron 1941-1942, Boeing Fortress 1 (B17c or B17e) were flown to Britain in the spring of 1941 but did not prove successful with Bomber Command. There were too many mechanical failures, the armament was inadequate and there were no long-range fighters available for daylight raids.*

A few were sent to the Middle East and the remainder were transferred to Coastal Command for reconnaissance and meteorological work. The belly gun was a 50" Browning gun in a ball turret which was called 'The Nookie.'

I met a lady who had an aunt in Wadebridge during the Second World War, whose son was a gunner in the Boeing Fortress. He said that the cold was the worst killer of all on night sortie. Once they were in the ball turret there was no way they could get out again in a hurry, and a lot of gunners were just blown away by ack-ack guns. His name was Walter, a young only son who lost his life during the war.

RODNEY'S STORY

Hello, I'm Rodney. I was a Cockney, born within the sound of Bow Bells.

I joined the RAF as a motorbike rider, because in Civvy Street I was a motorbike mechanic. My job was to see that all the motorbikes were ready to go at the first kick start. I rode an Enfield, which was my pride and joy, as a dispatch rider. I was often used to relay messages round the airfield, perhaps to different gun sites, also further afield if the wireless lines were out of action.

Most of my work was done at night – I enjoyed the night rides best, as I felt that I was the only one on the planet. I was a loner – of course, I had my band of mates and chums but I preferred my own company.

I was just eighteen when I joined up. My father and I ran a motorbike and car repair shop under one of the railway arches.

The Enfield was a good bike – no frills like now-a-days, no windscreen or leg protection either – we had to be tough to stand all weathers. The Enfield was made in Coventry and Birmingham before the war. They were all painted black and had the emblem of wings on the petrol tank. I was motorbike crazy. I lived, ate and slept on them and my Mum would say that if it had been possible, I would have been born on one.

I was stationed on a small airfield near Colchester in Essex. We had small airfields all over the place. Most Bomber Commands were on the east coast of England. I joined in 1942. I was always getting an ear bashing from the Sarge about my dirty, oily hands but what did he want, lily white hands? Cor Blimey, we were called 'grease monkeys.'

Let me tell you something about myself. I was short and stocky, with black hair and brown eyes. I had large hands and feet and fitted snugly on to the bike. I used to ride lying flat on the tank and, being short, I did this easily. I often got teased that my bike was my mistress as, to be crude, I always had my leg over her.

We had many a good laugh, mostly at others' misfortunes, but it was not meant unkindly. Girls? I never found enough time for them. I did have a girl once when I was young, before the war – she would ride pillion and hug me tight, but I didn't go to dances and the novelty soon wore off.

My nickname was Rod. I used to whistle a lot, trying to copy Ronny Ronalde – he really could whistle.

As I was telling you, I wore a leather bomber jacket, a leather cap with earmuffs which fastened under my chin, and goggles which were made of Perspex. I had my RAF uniform underneath. We were also issued with high-cuffed riding gauntlets. Part of my uniform was a gas mask, which we never went without. We had to learn to wear it, when necessary, as if it was a part of us. We could get 'put on a charge' if we were caught too many times without it.

I had a good mate called Timothy, who was always asking me questions. At fourteen he was too young to join up and lived on the base. He was a likeable lad – you could say he was my apprentice.

I like the clear, moonlit nights best, as I could ride without lights, well, not proper lights. We had a cover on the headlamp with a slit in it, so that only a small beam of light showed through. We always had to be wary of Jerry bombers.

It was nearly Christmas, and I had just gone home on compassionate leave as my Pa was ill – he suffered so much with his chest. On the night of 16th December there was a heavy bombing raid on London. Pa was in hospital, so Ma and I had to go down to our Anderson shelter at the bottom of the garden. We had just closed the door, lit the candle and said a prayer for Pa – I don't remember anything else, as our house and eight others in the row took a direct hit.

Then I was here, Cor Blimey mate, it was such a shock to both of us. Poor Pa didn't live long after that – Aunt Rosy, who lived in the next street, had to tell him the news. War is so dramatic. You never know what will happen or where, in the next hour or day.

Ta, luv, for letting me come and talk to you.

You will be getting a lot of us fellers telling you our own stories – making our own bit of history, which has not been told yet.

God bless you, and thank you. Rodney.

Rodney was short and stocky, about 5'6" tall, with dark hair and brown eyes. He had a tendency to be a bit scruffy and smoked cigarettes. He had a dry sense of humour. 18th August 1996

'MAYDAY, MAYDAY'

I never thought that I would ever, in my life, need that signal but here I was in the 'drink', my parachute was dragging me down and my life jacket wasn't giving me much support. Oh God, how cold I was, I was so numb with cold that I couldn't feel my fingers. My life jacket was called a Mae West.

There was the chance of being run down by a U-boat, or picked up by a minesweeper. I felt so utterly alone and tried to talk to myself, but I know it was all gibberish. Even my mind said 'Go to sleep' but I knew that I mustn't do that. This was my first mission and I was down somewhere in the Channel, in the darkest time before dawn. Fortunately, it wasn't raining and the sea was not too rough, but there was a nasty swell. The current was strong and I was being slowly sucked under the water, as I couldn't release the buckle of my parachute harness.

Suddenly, I remembered God – where was He? Why hadn't He brought someone to rescue me? I was too young to die and had an awful fear of water, as I couldn't swim. There was debris all round me, as parts of my Spitfire were still floating.

How did I get out of the cockpit? Oh yes, the plane had been hit, burst into flames and began spiralling down at a rapid pace. I had got out and the half opened parachute had cushioned my fall, but I still felt like an egg which had been dropped from a high building on to a hard surface – 'Mum, Mum' I heard myself call. She wouldn't know what had happened to me. Would anyone say I died bravely, fighting for my country, or would there just be a cable saying 'Missing.'

I thought I heard a throbbing sound and the water seemed to vibrate around me. I was so cold now and seemed to be drifting in and out of consciousness. How long had I been here – five minutes, five hours or five days? My parachute silk caught on something and there was an almighty wrench as it was torn off me. Now I was bobbing around like a broken cork in an old wine bottle.

Which direction was the sound coming from? Oh God, it was a sub – one of ours or a U-boat? I didn't mind who they were so long as I was out of the water.

'Please help me' I yelled, but no sound came out. Was I dreaming, or did I feel hands grab me and pull me out? I could hear voices, but not what was being said. I didn't really mind – I was out of the icy sea. Then I felt hot, stinging liquid poured down my throat – rum, I guess.

All the time I was in the water, I was too cold to know what injuries I had suffered – I just felt numb. Now, I couldn't stop shaking and ached all over. I drifted in and out of consciousness, blurred faces peered at me. I couldn't focus any more. Where was this pain coming from?

Then, a very strange feeling came over me – I was drifting above my body. Looking down, I saw that I was in a cot below decks. The British Navy had boats which came to rescue us airmen in the sea. My legs were gone, but I was more surprised than frightened. Everyone was standing around, there was an awful lot of blood, and then someone was giving me the last Rites, marking a cross on my forehead. I tried to call out 'I'm a Roman Catholic and I'll never get to Heaven unless this is done by a Catholic priest,' but it didn't seem to matter much. I felt no pain and didn't worry about anyone, or myself, any more. As I watched, my 'dog tags' were taken off, and I was put into a white bag for burial at sea. 'Oh no, not at sea – please not at sea, I hate the sea.' Then I don't remember any more.

I am over here now, and have been told that I will soon return to the earth plane once again. I flew a 'Spit' in November 1943, and it was my first and last flight in that cold, dark dawn of 15th November. I was twenty-one and my name was Teddy. I had looked forward to flying and earning my 'wings' but it all ended so suddenly, on my maiden flight. The chance of being picked up was very slim, so I suppose I was lucky in a way.

I felt it was appropriate for me to come today, having felt the pain of those left behind in a sea of misfortune.

Thank you for hearing and taking down my story.
God bless. Teddy.

> *Teddy was 5'8" tall, with a slim build, fair curly hair and blue eyes. He was very tidy and proud of his looks and clothes. He had a lovely smile, with even teeth.*
>
> *He brings others to me and is my link in the chain. 30th September 1996*
>
> *23/24 September 1996. Tragedy of two lads drowned while 'Boogie Boarding' (surfing) off the Cornish coast. It was dark and they got into difficulties near the rocks*

TOBRUK

My name is Johnny and I was twenty-one years old in may 1942. Oh, what a hellhole Tobruk was – the biggest beach I had ever seen. As a child, I can remember taking my first trip to the seaside with my bucket and spade, never thinking that I would spend a chunk of my life, and end my days, on this one.

On those war days I would spend so much time 'digging in' trenches in hot sand, hundreds of miles of it. It is God-awful stuff and got in everywhere – our hair, eyes, teeth and skin were covered in fine grains of the beastly stuff.

During a short spell at Aldershot for the basic 'bull', marching, orders and rules, I was thrown together with lads like myself. Being the first time away from home some of us were dreadfully homesick, but we had to be tough and pretend that we didn't care a damn. None of us knew when or where we would be transferred. I got the Tank Division with the Eighth Army near Tobruk.

The heat was the worst, as everything we touched was hot enough to take the skin off our hands. We could fry an egg, if we had one, on the tanks. Flies were the next worst thing, flies everywhere. We would have to fight our way through swarms of the things, on our food, our clothes and the next bite we would start to eat. If it wasn't the flies during the day, it was mosquitoes at night. There were all sorts of nasty things in the desert to bite us. We had warm water to drink and I longed for a pint of beer. Our food and water were rationed but we had plenty of Woodbines – only by smoking were we able to keep the flies away.

Those were long, hot days sitting under camouflage netting with our tanks, waiting for the night manoeuvres. Even then, it was dreadful having to climb down into the sardine tin of a tank. Oh God, how hot and stuffy it was – the sweat used to run down my brow and blind me like tears. I saw a few Arabs with their camels, but we made a point of never letting them know where we were, as spies were everywhere. We were quite a large Battalion with a hospital and nurses under canvas.

We also had Monty, who would come by with other 'big wigs,' all crisply turned out with battle plans on paper. Their war was on paper – ours was in the desert. We were the ones who fought their war for them and we were expendable. They would look so calm and cool but we men took the full force of the fighting.

As twilight darkened the sky and the heat shimmered its last mirage in the half dark, we would fuel up and head out on our mission. I felt so trapped in the tank, though we could drive anywhere and over any terrain in them. The desert nights were so cold − it was from one extreme to the other.

There were jerries everywhere, with planes scouting for convoys − us − and we were sitting targets, no match for the planes. Over the noise of the tanks we could hear very little else.

Just before Tobruk fell we were spread out in a long line, rumbling on, when suddenly we were under fire, our tank guns blasting off. My tank took a direct hit and burst into flames. Most of the crew got out, but I was trapped by my legs. Oh Mary, Mother of God, the heat, the flames − I couldn't breathe and my hair and clothes were on fire 'Help, Help me.' The smoke was black and oily, my skin melting like a candle and all I could do was sit there. Then there was a big explosion and it was all over for me, though it might have been the smoke that actually finished me.

Then it was so quiet and I felt no more panic or pain. It took me a long time to come to terms with being burnt alive. We had often come across Germans sprawled over their burning tanks − I can say 'Poor blighters' now as I know what they went through. Those scars are now gone − I am just as young and handsome as I was before those dark days of the war.

My tank had *Lily Marlene* painted on her side and we had been through a lot together, but our luck ran out on those hot, barren seas of sand, flies and dust in North Africa.

Thank you for allowing me to come through. This is the first time I have made contact and told my story. God bless. Johnny.

Johnny was short 5'3" and thick set, with dark wavy hair and a strong jaw line. He had large hands, dark hazel eyes, a cheeky smile and wore glassed for reading. Sue Searle thinks that Johnny was her uncle, Johnny Toft.

The Battle of Tobruk, May − June 1942 was a battle in the North African Campaign of World War 2, an Axis victory that exposed Egypt to the threat of German occupation. Tobruk, the focus of much bitter fighting since its capture by the British in January 1941, finally fell after months of fighting, to the Afrika Corps under the command of Rommel, on 20th June. 33,000 British troops were taken prisoner. It was recaptured in November 1942.

FJORDS

My name is Andersen and I am Norwegian. In 1942 I was trained in sabotage, as I knew the country, mountains and fjords well. I was used as a guide to lead the bravest of British soldiers into the fjords to sabotage the Heavy Water factories, which the Germans had built beneath the mountains, at the head of the fjords.

Our training was strenuous and only the fittest were selected. We had to learn to walk on skis over heavy terrain, carried all our equipment on our backs and wore white. Everything was white except for our goggles, which were black to protect our eyes against the glare of the snow. Snow blindness was easy to get – if we got complacent and forgot to wear the goggles we were returned to base.

We had to have real guts, as we were often dropped by parachute behind enemy lines. The enemy in my country, my beloved Norway – how I hated the Bosch. Before the War I had been a mountaineer and a guide, so I knew all the pitfalls that lay ahead of us. Patience was our main requirement, for lying in wait and picking the right moment. We were taught stealth and how to kill without making a sound, in hand to hand combat.

I led a group of six of the finest men I have ever had the privilege to know and work with. They were young, fearless and even reckless at times. Quite often I would lose a couple of them to Bosch snipers. As we were all in white, we thought we were invisible – far from it. The Bosch fired at anything that moved, regardless of whether it was a worker or a saboteur! We had to have eyes in the back of our heads and were meant to watch each other's backs, but this was not always possible.

We had to leave our comrades behind if they were wounded. Each man knew what would befall him if he was caught but this was part of the special assignment we had vowed to carry out, and we knew the risks.

Our target that night was a large Heavy Water factory with a rocket site. We had been primed with as much information as we could get from our spies inside, but we were still going in blind. A blizzard had been blowing all day and we had travelled several kilometres on foot, arriving above the fjord and factory by early afternoon. We had to abseil down the side of the mountain and I had chosen a spot where I hoped we could not be seen by the sentries and gunners, who were in gun emplacements set into the side of the mountain.

The time we had chosen was 4.30 p.m. just as the day shift came out and the night shift went in. We were very cold and exhausted after battling against the unexpected blizzard. We anchored our ropes, put on our harnesses and started to descend. It was now dark, but suddenly searchlights lit up the side of the mountain – again, we were not expecting so much light. The first three descended safely and I went down with the other three, being the last to descend.

We had to hide our white camouflage gear and change into clothes similar to those worn by the factory workers. All went well, though it was a bit scary, as I was sure we had been picked up by the searchlights. We had to meet up with four of our co-workers who had got themselves on to the night shift. Many of these were prisoners of war who were transported by train under guards with dogs, at all times. The Bosch never counted the workers at night – they were always in such a hurry to close the doors. So, we got in, mingling with the men and women workers.

I was surprised to see the vastness of the factory, so brightly lit. Bit by bit we slipped into the shadows and set the fuses of our bombs, where we thought they would cause as much damage as possible. Suddenly, an air raid siren went off and we were all rounded up. The Bosch were always so unpredictable and this was where the trouble started. In fact, it was a German plane and not a British one, but there was panic everywhere.

Then came the reprisals, for every time the air raid sirens went off the Bosch were so trigger happy that they picked out thirty of at random, and shot a few. Not all thirty were shot but no one knew who would be chosen. This was to teach us a lesson, as the Germans would not tolerate anyone contemplating sabotage.

Unfortunately, I was one of those chosen, so I never knew if our sabotage that night was successful, or if the men in my charge got away safely. I never thought that I would end my days like this. I could see the horror in the eyes of my men, but we dared not give each other away. I was twenty-six years old when I lost my life.

I loved my Norway, the land of the northern lights that painted the snowfields in blues, greens and pinks like the brush of a magic artist painting a rainbow.

Thank you, my friend, for finally allowing me to come through; I have been trying for quite a while. I knew you heard me, as I heard you say 'I keep getting Norway, fjords and snow' but you were not well, so I waited. Now you have it all. God bless.

Andersen was 6'3" tall, well built and athletic. He had a mop of blond hair, large hands and feet and green/hazel eyes which twinkled.
Received 8.1.1997.

KUALA LUMPUR

Hello, I'm Kristine. I joined the Army as a Q.A. (Queen Alexandra Nurse), when nurses were needed to serve abroad and on troopships. I felt my quiet days as a nurse in a cottage hospital were coming to an end. From starting as a mere nurse − well, you know what I mean − I had just become a Sister. My friend, Susie, and I joined up on one of my days off. We enlisted as lieutenants, dressed in grey dresses, red capes and wide white caps. My, how proud we were − heads turned and wolf whistles followed us, though we were not allowed to wear our nursing uniforms when off duty.

We embarked at Southampton, final destination Malaya. We were thrown in at the deep end, so to speak, as this was the first time we had really been away from home. We were lucky that we were both posted to the same military hospital in Kuala Lumpur. Oh, what a beautiful country it is, so lush and green with exotic, perfumed flowers.

At that time, Malaya was still British with only distant rumours of the Japanese. Although our troops were fighting the Japs in the jungle, we never thought that they would over-run us like ants.

So, for eighteen months we were treating servicemen, some severely wounded, who were taken home to England when strong enough, never to fight again. Then, one morning we woke up to a sound that we had previously only heard in the far distance − gunfire. There was panic, shouting and slaughter − the Japs had invaded unexpectedly from up country and there were swarms of them everywhere.

The first thing we had to do was evacuate the hospital. The walking wounded were on foot and the rest were carried on stretchers. There was no time to pack, so I had to leave everything behind. How tired I was, as I had been rushed off my feet since dawn. Susie and I were separated. She might have boarded a train bound for Singapore and the docks, but I never saw her again. We were lined up, rifle butts in our backs and shouted at in an unrecognisable language, so I was really frightened. All the women, children and babies were in separate groups from the men. We were pushed and shoved, a bedraggled bunch of pathetic women.

The hospital was by then empty – all our equipment left behind. We were on the march and walked for days. When the old fell, they were shot beside the path. We were thirsty, hungry and so weary. We carried the children on our backs in turn, taking the youngest first. After about four days we finally saw a camp ahead of us, deep in the jungle, with a high barbed wire fence, little huts in rows and guards at the gate. We had started out as a group of thirty-seven but, on arrival, a head count showed only thirty one, as we had lost three adults and three babies, the new-born being the first to go.

We were lined up and counted twice a day, which was to become routine for the rest of my life. Our food was rice, and more rice, with far-from-clean water to drink. I was the only one with medical knowledge, so I was put in charge of the sick. Life in the camp was horrendous – days dragged into weeks, then months and finally years. A few more women arrived from time to time during the war. How were any of us to survive with no Red Cross parcels or letters? Did anyone know where we were? I feared not.

We were a forgotten group of people, living in bamboo shacks behind high barbed wire fences. Dysentery, malaria and diseases from rat bites killed one or two of us every month, until our numbers dwindled to a handful. We had to go out in working parties every day and just to get out of the gate was an escape for the mind. Our dead were buried outside the wire, row after row of them. At first, we tried to mark the graves with crosses and names, but this became pointless in the end, as no one would find us. We heard some rumours of rescue but nothing ever happened.

The monsoon came again with its stench and everything, even our mats, were wet through so that we slept on the ground. The rice was always full of weevils and I used to joke: 'Protein today!' We lost our dignity, pride and hope but hung on to our memories. We were a pathetic sight – dirty, in rags, with sores and ringworm, whilst out guards had clean water to shower with, clean clothes and decent food. I had given up thoughts of rescue years before and did not expect to see a white man again. We lived on our memories of husbands, lovers, fathers and sons. The Japs despised us as women, so vastly inferior to men.

Some of the younger girls, although warned against it, fraternised with the guards, which brought miscarriages and disease to add to our plight. I had worms very badly, so my stomach was distended and painful to touch, although I was losing weight and couldn't stand for long. We ran out of everything except salt so we saved our weekly ration for washing sores. I felt that my time was running out, and that I would never know freedom again, although there was much excitement among the Japs and more head counts than usual.

My end was near. When I coughed, which I did often, the pain was dreadful and I asked God to release me from the hell I was in. Early one morning, I saw my Gran standing at the end of my mat, smiling – she had come for me. I had often heard patients talking to their Mum or Dad just before they died, so I was not afraid. The year was 1944 and I was twenty-seven years old.

Thank you for hearing my story – I seem to have chatted for so long but I had to give you all the details, so that people will know that wars must end. God bless.

The war in Malaya ended in the summer of 1945, after the atomic bomb was dropped on Japan by America. Received on March 3rd. 1997.

Auschwitz

Shalom. Hello, my friend, my name is Samuel and I am twelve years old. When the Nazis came we had to live in a ghetto. Rounded up at the beginning of the war, we had to leave our homes and were packed like rats into dreadful conditions, sometimes three families in one flat or room.

I was the middle child of the family, with two brothers older than myself and two sisters younger. We lived in fear and held our prayer meetings in secret, for fear of being reported. There were monthly raids when families were rounded up, taken away in lorries and trains to concentration camps, and never heard of again.

Father was a goldsmith and we boys were all learning the same trade. One night, we heard marching boots screams and gunfire and we didn't have time to hide. My two brothers were the first to be caught in our family, and the next to go, were my mother and sisters. We never saw them again. My father was distraught with anguish, but I was hiding with him beneath the floorboards under the bed, so once again I had been saved.

I was only eight years old when all this Jewish trouble started, and wondered how much longer we could survive. Our family was being eaten away bit by bit. Then the fatal day came when my father and I were caught. I hung on to his coat, for fear of being torn away from him. With rifle butts in our ribs we were pushed into lorries. The place bristled with Germans − such angry people, and we could see the hate and disgust in their eyes at having to touch us, as though we were unclean lepers, and the fear that they might catch something from us.

I remember that it was a cold day in December, with flurries of snow falling from a heavy, grey sky. There followed a long train journey standing crushed in a cattle truck. We couldn't see out and very little air got in so, being small, I was nearly suffocated. After what seemed like a lifetime the train slowed down and panic started to surge through the wagons. The doors were opened and a blast of icy wind blew in on our hot cramped bodies.

We heard shouts to get out and we fell on to the hard ground, many on top of each other. Father had one arm round me, holding me close to him. Then one of the Germans shouted, 'Do you have a trade? All those who have a trade step forward.' So Father stepped forward, taking me with him.

At first, people were hesitant about making the first move, so we were separated from the rest. 'Trade?' 'Goldsmith with my son, he's very good,' Father said, so we were marched off away from our comrades, not through the high gates but through a smaller gate to the side of the compound. There were thousands of Jews. I had never seen so many people in all my life. They didn't all speak German – some were Polish, some Hungarian and others Slavs.

We were pushed into a long shed. It was very dark inside and it took a few moments for our eyes to adjust. The first thing I noticed was the smell – I can't describe it but it was the smell of fear. Cases were piled high and people were sorting out belongings, fur coats, shoes, glasses, books, candlesticks, food and jewellery. Then I saw a pile of small gold pieces, which I was later told were gold fillings from teeth. We were told to sort them out, as they were to be melted down and made into gold rings and jewellery for the Nazis. At first, Father didn't want to touch them but a rifle butt in the back soon changed his mind.

A special smelting kiln was produced and Father and I started to work. I was a very sensitive child and when I touched those gold teeth I felt fear and death. On the floor beside us, in the corner, was a pile of toys and dolls and next to them a heap of women's hair. This was the death camp, Auschwitz. A small electric light bulb swung over our heads, casting grotesque shadows on the walls around us, like the ghosts of the murdered Jews.

Year after year, the pile of gold never seemed to get any smaller. We slept and ate little and all the time it snowed grey ash from belching chimneys, and the smell of death hung like a shroud around us. Father became ill and he had a heart attack on the evening of my eleventh birthday. He was taken away, they said to a hospital, but I never saw him again. I was very gifted and made a heavily engraved gold plate, set with emeralds and rubies, as a gift for some senior officer's wedding. He wanted the Nazi symbol engraved around the edge. I had to draw it first and take it to be inspected. At first they would stand with whips in their hands, demanding that I worked faster but I used to say 'If you make me work faster I will make mistakes' so they soon left me alone.

I made three of those plates of solid gold, a priceless piece of work, but every time I melted down those gold teeth my heart would cry out with pain. Next, they wanted a goblet studded with gemstones. I no longer made the signet rings with skulls on them, as there was so much gold.

Rumours ran around like wildfire that we would soon be liberated, that the Russians were coming, but day after day nothing happened. The chimneys stopped belching out grey ash, starving people were made to dig deep trenches, and then one evening there was gunfire. It went on and on, well into the night, and the compound began to empty of the starving people.

Again rumours were spread that the Nazis were trying to cover up the slaughter of the Jews by burying them in those trenches.

Then one day we woke to silence. Our jailers were gone and we were left without food or water behind the high barbed wire fences. We heard the rumble of far off tanks and then young army officers were there and we were liberated. I was just twelve years old and was nearly blind, as I had not seen sunlight for four years, shut behind heavy shed doors working with gold, working to keep myself alive.

There were many other children left when the Russians came to liberate us. We were starving; just bones in rags, and bodies lay everywhere. Men and women once young and full of life were now just rotting corpses. Many soldiers were crying as they gave us water and small amounts of food.

It took some time for the compound to be cleared of bodies. Some records were found of who they were and how many there were, but most had been burnt. We were taken to a big army camp where doctors came to examine us. I was very sick – they said I had consumption as I was coughing up blood and could hardly stand. The Russians were kind, but came too late to save most of us.

I had survived over four years in the Auschwitz death camp, living on my wits and putting my skills to use to save my life. Father was murdered and so were the rest of my family all those years ago. I was now free but death caught up with me.

I came today because I felt that I should add my story to history, and I thank you for hearing me out. I sometimes hear people on earth asking when we holocaust victims will return. Well, there is no time in the Spirit world and we must be helped to come to terms with our traumatic imprisonment and deaths before we can return.

I did not die in a gas chamber, but as a free child, so maybe it was easier for me to return now.

God bless, Shalom, peace be with you. Samuel.

Received 26th April 2002

Hurricane

Hello, I am Timothy. I flew a Hurricane in 1942. Our base was in Kent, on the coast, though this was not the first airbase on which I had been stationed. Our first was badly bombed by Jerry so we had to be relocated. I lost friends every week and hated that dreadful war

I had twenty hours flying time under my belt and was one of the few hard liners who had flown a lot of missions.

The Hurricane was a good, sturdy plane with guns on the wings, but not as fast or agile as a Spit. I say 'Spit' but you know that's what we called the Spitfires.

Our missions were over France to Germany, flying in formation at high altitudes. We never took our boots off when we were on standby, and our bomber jackets were on but never fastened until we were ready to fly. We used to sit and read the newspaper or a book, flicking through the pages where someone else might have marked something but never returned to it. Quite honestly, I never remembered what I read. The words were meaningless to me, as our ears were always waiting for 'Scramble!'

I had adopted the airfield's mascot, a lovely old dog which had belonged to Leader One. He had been shot down so, as I had always loved dogs, I took over and tried to give him comfort, as he was pining so much. He could hear our planes coming home long before we could. He could also tell if they were Jerries, and would then start to bark and kick up a racket several minutes before we got the word 'Thirty at three thousand feet, coming from the east', so we valued his sharp ears.

I could never rest – my nerves were taut and my mind on my little family in Hampshire. I had been married for two years and we had a little daughter called Emily, who was just a year old. She was my pride and joy and I hated being so far away from them, especially when there was so much bombing. My home leave had been cancelled at the last minute – much disappointment was felt by all of us, as we had been looking forward to a weekend off the field, in the arms of our loved ones.

Love in wartime was something we had to snatch – precious moments to hold on to until the next time. I remembered the sweet taste of Sally's lips, the tears she fought back so that I wouldn't see them, that long last hug and the spring fragrance of her auburn hair, before I had to go. Fighting back the tears, I'd give them a quick wave and blow a kiss – I hated to leave them behind, but this was war. After my last forty eight-hour leave, two months ago, I was longing for the moment when I could hold them again.

Then I was running across the airfield, doing up my jacket and struggling into my parachute harness. This was an uncomfortable thing to sit on but could be a lifesaver. I had not had to bail out yet, but I had a premonition that this mission was not going to go as planned. I just couldn't get my girls out of my mind and had to fight the memory away. After a quick prayer, I checked that the chocks were away and almost automatically I was in the air, looking down on the airfield in the light of the spring sunset far below.

We were up, eyes searching the sky, flying in formation. I was Leader One now, call up the stragglers to keep in close ranks. Then we banked and peeled off, two to the right and two to the left. I thought of Vera Lynn's song *Over the white cliffs of Dover* as we left England far behind. There, ahead of us, were the Luftwaffe – big German bombers droning towards us across the Channel. We came down out of the sky, firing our guns. 'Got him!' one, shouted. 'Watch out, Charlie, one behind you – I've been hit!' 'Bale out, man, bale out!' I screamed, glancing over my shoulder. I had also been hit – smoke was pouring out of my engine and the tail had also been badly damaged. I was losing control.

Then I was in flames – I couldn't open the cockpit and everything was on fire. I was blinded by smoke, oil and flames. What were those terrifying screams? Were they mine? 'Not this way, Lord Jesus, not this way please.'

Then all went quiet and I saw a vision of cool, green fields and Sally when we were courting. I wasn't frightened anymore and my life flashed before my eyes. I don't remember any more, no pain or panic. I was floating far above the clouds, away from the noise of the war – I was going home. I met up with Teddy, you know Teddy, and he has brought me to you.

You are doing a grand job, my lass, a grand job. So many thousands of us died in mid air, blown to pieces, never to be found. This was my own horrendous experience. At least someone will read this when you get our stories published and someone; somewhere will say, 'He was my boy, my son' and thank you.

Greater rewards will come to you, for you listen to us 'lost ones' and we can't thank you enough. I passed on Easter Monday 1943, aged 25 years.

God bless you. Timothy.

Received March 9th. 1997.

Dunkirk

My name was Andrew and I was twenty-one years old when I stood, smart in my military uniform, waiting to be taken across the Channel, with our Expeditionary Force, to France. It was 1940 and rumours spread amongst the troops that we were being used as a toy army, to go in to test the situation. This war was going to be over by Christmas – everybody said so.

It was the proudest day of my life as I waved goodbye to my wife. I was a proud British soldier, off to war to fight for my country. We were landed on the north west coast of France and then started to march inland, pushing back stray units of Germans. We thought that if this was all the war was going to be, it would be a push over. Never did I think, for one moment, that we would be turning and running for home, with our tails between our legs.

It was humiliating and I hated what the British soldier now stood for. We had lost face, dignity and pride and were considered cowards. We felt that the Germans were laughing at us for running home to Mummy's apron strings. I was utterly ashamed of being a part of the British army.

We were pushed back up the coast of France to Dunkirk. There were about five and a half thousand of us, and this included some French soldiers who were never really ready to fight for their country – cowards! They were prepared to hand their country over to the Germans. Later, of course, France suffered greatly.

We stood up to our waists in the icy sea, each pushing to be the next to get a place on any small boat which had rallied to the call to rescue us. There were narrow boats, dinghies and even small boats with tiny engines, which could only take three or four of us. From the air, we looked like a mass of dark ants swarming over the beach and into the sea. All the time, the Germans were bombing us and firing on us – where was our air cover? The casualties were terrible.

That was where I got it. The sea was full of soldiers and we had to sit on the beach and wait for our turn. There was no protection – time and again the German planes flew over us, shooting at random, the bullets hitting the beach with a thump and a spray of sand. I had been on the beach for most of the day Why couldn't we fight back? We had to run over and take the dog tags off dying soldiers; as I sat with a young lad whose stomach had been shot to bits, as no one ever wanted to die alone. There were shouts for orderlies and medics.

Then I also was hit. It happened so fast and then I was standing on the beach with all my dead comrades. Soldiers walked through us – couldn't they see us? No bullets could ever hurt us again. I have felt for so long the dishonour that we all experienced, after we had been told that we had to fight for England. There was the shame of running away – we should have stayed, as there were enough of us to fight back. Perhaps, if Dunkirk had not taken place, the war would not have lasted so long.

I am at long last coming to terms with what my fate ordained for me. I was an angry young man, full of resentment and hurt pride. Now I know that there was nothing I could have done about it. It was a cruel twist of fate, and my destiny.

I never lived to see the babe my wife was carrying, but I know I can watch the little one grow up. I passed on the red curly hair! I was 5'6" tall and slim, with bright red curly hair.

What a waste of life when the war snatched us away – a whole generation snuffed out in the blink of an eye, for the second time. I have come to terms with it now.

God bless you and thank you. Please let my family know that I have made contact with you through Teddy, and that I watch over them all.

Teddy was a Spitfire pilot and is my link with those on the Other Side. He was posted 'Missing, presumed dead'. This might have been Andrew Le Grice. I was asked to see whether I could contact him. The young man is not Andrew Le Grice.
Received in March 1997.

THE SWEET SMELL of DEATH

My name is David and I was nineteen years old when I went 'home.'

The sweet smell of death hung like a heavy, depressing cloud all around me – it was the first and last sickly smell I would remember. I couldn't hear or see anything, as I had been deafened and blinded by the explosion of a shell close to the hollow in which I lay. I was pressed hard into the mud of our dug out, unable to move, and the only sense I had left was my sense of smell. I suppose you could have said that I was a living dead man.

Next, I remember rough hands lifting me on to a stretcher and being jostled and humped over rough terrain. Then I was put down on the ground, presumably under canvas, as I could no longer feel the rain on my face. I was bewildered and frightened. There was someone near me and I could smell Lysol, then felt a jab – morphine, I expect. I was in a completely silent, dark world and with my two major senses gone I was terrified about what to expect next.

I felt no more pain and seemed to be drifting somewhere out of reach of everyone else. I suppose I was semi-conscious and in deep shock. The sweet smell of death still hung around me like a damp blanket.

My mind went back to the green hills of Devon, the red earth, cows in the meadows and larks hanging in the air. I was young again, running through the hay fields chasing butterflies. I had been an only child and spent many a long day on my own, sometimes sitting in the branches of my favourite tree, or lying flat on my tummy on the bank, trying to tickle the trout. I lived in a make-believe world of my own. Now I was there again, the colours were bright and vibrant and the birdsong, especially the nightingale, throbbingly beautiful. I was going home.

It was 1944 and I had been on a special mission to France, behind enemy lines – all hush, hush. We had been ambushed by the jerries and cut off from our main group. I lay in my dugout for what felt like two days before I was rescued, but I don't know who picked me up. There wasn't much anyone could have done for me by then.

When I was on the Earth, I had always planned to join the Ministry as a priest, but now I was just an ordinary soldier, alone and frightened in another land.

Thank you for hearing me. I'm sorry that I disturbed you with that smell, but I didn't know how to contact you in any other way. Now that you have taken down my story, I will remove the smell of death which filled my nostrils and lingered on while I hovered between the two worlds. It's strange how that smell scared you, so that you asked for it to be taken away. I didn't know that you could smell it so strongly.

How else could I contact you? Roses and lilies also came to your mind – old, dying flowers at a graveside. At least we have now had contact with each other.

God bless and goodnight. Teddy sent me to you. Thank you for hearing me out.

David, nicknamed Tich, was 5'3" tall, with a slim, small frame, dark hazel eyes and a shock of unruly fair hair which was always over his eyes. He was wiry, with little flesh on his bones, so his Gran used to ask 'Mother, don't you ever feed this boy?'

From 9.30am on Thursday 9th October 1997, I smelt a sweet, sickly smell on my left side as I sat at the table. I lit a candle and asked for it to be taken away. I also asked what it was, and was told 'It is the sweet smell of death,' and that someone wanted to make contact.

I had company that morning, so it wasn't until 3.45pm that I was able to sit down, pencil and paper ready, and David came through. When I had finished writing, the smell went away.

THE BURMA RAILWAY

I, (Lawrence) and Edmond were identical twins. We both joined up in the army in 1940 and were posted to Malaya with our platoon. Our main objective was to search out the Japs in the jungle. Jungles to us were a nightmare, as we were from Civvy Street in England. I was studying Law and Edmond was doing Civil Law, but we were not working together as it was difficult to work for the same firm. We were as alike as two peas in a pod, so decided to work in different parts of London. We were so close that we thought the same thoughts at the same time, and at the end of the day we would compare notes and find that we had done the same things, even down to having identical food for lunch.

Now we were sweltering in the most God-forsaken place on earth. The greatest number of trees we had ever seen together were in Hyde Park. We had to cope with swamps, leeches, snakes and large mosquitoes, whose humming was so irritating.

We didn't really want to enlist but we both thought that it would be an adventure and decided to give it a try. How dreadfully wrong we were – it was no picnic and certainly no adventure – it was hell.

The tropical jungles were a nightmare. We couldn't just walk in a straight line, but had to hack our way through a dense mass of vines, bamboos and impossible undergrowth and seldom saw the sky. A lot of our comrades were taken ill with malaria, yellow fever and dysentery. Flies and nasty creepy crawlies were everywhere. I didn't have a dry shirt on my back for more than five minutes, as we were always soaked with sweat from the humidity. We must have been a smelly lot, but as we all smelt the same we couldn't tell the difference.

We were out on patrol one early morning, trying to find the Japs, who were so at home in the jungle and moved around with ease. They made tunnels in the undergrowth, popping up in the most unexpected places, even behind us. We used to stumble along, falling over dead trees, tripping on undergrowth and falling into swamps. I'm sure the Japs could hear us long before they saw us. Snipers were the worst. This is where Edmond got it – he was shot in the back of the head and died instantly, right beside me.

It was the most devastating thing that had ever happened to us, being parted like this, but then the most extraordinary thing happened. He was standing in front of me saying 'Come on, brother, don't stand there, drop to your knees, hide and follow me. I will never leave you.' I was blinded by tears. How could Ed be there dead beside me and yet talking to me? I put out my hand to touch him, thinking I was dreaming, but he was real enough – there were two of him. I was the only one who could see him and talk to him. Later, I was told that the bond between us was so strong that even if the shell of his body was gone, his soul had not.

He had always been the leader of our gang as children, the one to do the most daring of jumps, swings and shinning up ropes. I tackled these with caution and got there in the end but always a little behind him. Now I was on my own, as far as the rest of the men were concerned, although I wasn't really. To them I began to act strangely, talking to myself and living in a world of my own and they used to steer away from me. I often volunteered to do point duty so that I could talk to Ed and I was never alone after that.

After a few weeks of jungle fighting we were out-numbered, one afternoon, by a platoon of Japs in a ravine. There was a lot of shooting and many were killed on both sides before we were taken prisoner. We marched for days until, somewhere in the middle of nowhere, we were pushed into a camp where more bedraggled prisoners welcomed us. Conditions were very bad and they all looked ill and very thin. The camp was in a clearing in the jungle, where the first sun I had seen for weeks hurt our eyes. The glare and heat were so different from the darkness of the jungle. There was a different kind of dampness now, hot and humid but with no shade.

Rice was our daily ration and one cup of water morning and evening, if we were lucky. I was working in a labour gang, building the Burma railway. We worked long hours, from dawn to dusk and were whipped if we stopped working. If we fell ill and dropped beside the track, our mates would pick us up and cause a distraction until we could begin to work again. Some were shot, depending on the guards, some of whom were kinder than others. Our comradeship grew strong as we protected each other. Some of the men had been in that camp for a year, but out of the hundreds who arrived there, only half remained and only a quarter went out to work.

Ulcers were one of the main causes of illness. We did have a doctor who did what he could for us, but we were not allowed to linger in camp for long, always pushed out to work on that damned railway. Cutting through the jungle was easy compared with cutting by hand, with pick and shovel, through hillsides and deep ravines. Our sabotage was to 'go slow' which infuriated the Japs. We lost or broke off bolts, so that only half the rails were held firmly in position. We got quite good at thinking up schemes to slow down, or put a stop to, our work.

All the time, Ed worked beside me. I was warned many times not to talk to myself, as the Japs wouldn't tolerate madness, so I learnt to talk mentally to Ed and he talked to me in this way also. I fell silent and he would often suggest ideas which I could put forward. Sometimes I saw other 'dead' mates walking between us. They would lift a hand in greeting but seldom said anything. The poor lost souls didn't want to be on their own, and who could blame them? I was a prisoner for about four years and during that time our parents never knew what had happened to us. We had no contact with the outside world and received no Red Cross parcels from home.

One night, I woke in a cold sweat, shaking and screaming out. Ed was kneeling beside me, saying 'Hang in there, brother.' I had a very bad attack of malaria and was hallucinating, seeing Mother and Father and ourselves riding in Hyde Park and playing as children – Edmond and I were young again. I don't know how long I was ill but I never went back to work on the railway. As each day passed I could see less and I went blind. I knew that Ed was with me, as I could see him even with my eyes closed. I drifted in and out of consciousness and eventually could hear nothing.

Then, all of a sudden, I was whizzing down a long, bright tunnel with a brilliant light ahead of me. Ed was holding my hand and saying 'We are free. Let's go, let's leave, hurry, it's wonderful over here.' It took a little while for me to realise that I was dead. I felt free of pain and I could see again. The light didn't hurt my eyes and, best of all we were together again, as in the early days before that dreadful war. Edmond had stayed to protect me and had earned his freedom and rest.

I want to thank you for hearing my story. I seem to have told you so much, but of the two of us I was always the scholarly one. Edmond passed over on May 3rd 1940 and I joined him on May 3rd 1944, just before our twenty-seventh birthday.

God bless and keep you safe. You are doing a job which is well worth while, with great rewards to come. Lawrence and Edmond.

Received on February 4th 1999.

YVETTE
Mademoiselle de la Nuit

Hello, I am Yvette. When the Germans invaded France I was a 'Lady of the Night,' therefore I thought that my trade would come in useful for the Underground Movement. I could flirt with the Germans quite freely and they got used to seeing me around in unexpected places, even after curfew when no one was allowed to be out on the streets. I got quite a reputation with my fellow countrymen, who despised me and the work I did, but at that time more and more British airmen were being shot down over France and we had to get them back to England. So, at the age of twenty, I began work as a member of the Underground Movement.

I was born in Vichy, in the south of France. By listening to conversations and pillow talk, I found out when army platoons and regiments would be on the move, and was able to pass on this valuable information to the Underground. At first we were badly organised and found that we had one or two collaborators among us.

In those early days, one or two airmen would be rescued by farmers and hidden. Then word would come 'We have a special package to be delivered to someone.' As time passed, of course, some were captured or a plan would fail. It was on one of these occasions that a collaborator informed on me.

On the night in question, I was hanging around a café in the square where I usually made my conquests for a few Deutsche Marks, when a group of soldiers marched in and arrested me. I was taken to a house which had been commandeered by the Germans as their HQ in that small town, and was questioned by many men who had bedded me. Their language was appalling as they showed their true colours. Where once sweet words of love were whispered in my ear, there were now words of disgust and hatred and some even spat at me.

I was bound to a chair with my arms behind me and my legs tied. I was tortured, hit, whipped and gang raped, again and again but I never said anything, nor said that I had anything to do with the

Underground. I don't know how long I was roped to the chair, nor how long I lay on the stone floor of the cellar. If my mother had seen me she would never have known me. My pretty face was cut, my long hair torn my eyes blackened and my lips swollen and broken.

I reached a stage where, if this torture had gone on any longer, I would have confessed to anything. My arm was broken and they threw me around like a rag doll.

Then, one night I was stripped of most of my clothing, dragged out, put into a car and driven for many kilometres in the dark and cold to a fir wood. There I was told 'You are free to go' and as I stumbled away I heard them laughing, the click of a pistol and then I was shot in the back. As I fell on to the sweet, damp fir needles a great lightness and peace seemed to cover me, and I felt myself lifted in the arms of an angel. I was at peace at last. Mon Dieu, it was wonderful not to feel any more pain.

I had to get in touch with you as I also rescued airmen – like your work, as you rescue young servicemen and women. I just wanted to tell you my sad little story. Like many of your people I was never found, but so many of us loyal French men and women went in this way. Thank you for listening to me. I came through to you just after your healing, but you were certainly not expecting to hear from me, a French 'Lady of the Night.' We all played a part in that awful war. I passed on January 16th 1940.

> *Yvette was 4'9" tall with a petite frame. She had dark brown eyes and black hair, and wore a dark felt hat at a jaunty angle on her head. She passed at twenty-one years old.*

ANDY, MORRIS and CLAUD'S STORY

My name was Morris; I was twenty-five years old with green eyes, mousy brown hair and about 5'8" tall. Claud was a year older than me, a very quiet bloke who was always spouting poetry. He was a scholar and well read – I think he knew all the poems in his little book off by heart. He was twenty-six, of medium build and suffered badly from the gear he had to carry. The straps made red marks on his shoulders and I sometimes rubbed surgical spirit on them to toughen them up. Then there was Andy, the baby of the three of us. He was just nineteen, tall and lanky with little flesh on his bones, but always hungry. We looked after each other as the best way to stay alive.

We were in France, after the disastrous evacuation at Dunkirk, and were the next lot to go in. We were on patrol on August 1st 1941 and our task was to rout out snipers who were in a bell tower, picking us off one by one. There had been hand-to-hand fighting most of the day, with no time for a break for a cigarette, and we had to have eyes in the back of our heads.

It had been a long, hot day and the snipers were particularly bad – they seem to be everywhere. We had cornered a pocket of Jerries in a small hamlet which the French had left, and were trying to do our job without air cover. Our aircraft would normally have been overhead, helping us to drive them out, but that day there was low cloud which blotted out a clear view. It was a sultry day and most uncomfortable – our uniforms were soaked with sweat and covered with dust, and my mouth felt like the inside of a birdcage.

We three musketeers had been together from the beginning, since we boarded the boat to take us across the Channel. We had found a quiet corner and played Cribbage – anything to take our minds off what lay ahead of us. It was about 3pm in the afternoon when Claud was hit. God knows where the bullet came from – one minute he was crouched down, running along beside a wall and the next he was down on the ground with a bullet in his back. I managed to pull him into a doorway, but he had been hit in the heart. I wept silently as I said 'Goodbye' and mumbled what I could remember of the Lord's Prayer. He would have liked that.

Then, I was on the move again trying to catch up with Andy, who was hiding just ahead of me. I told him about Claud and he was visibly shaken. 'Oh, God' he said 'I'll be next.' He carried a wireless set and we wondered whether we should report our position and tell the rest of the battalion that we were under fire, and taking casualties. Someone ran past us, was shot and lay moaning in the dusty street.

We decided to stay put, in our relatively safe position, as we had a good view up and down the street and it was cool inside the ruins of the house. There were German tanks, with many dead bodies lying around them.

Then we were both hit. Andy was first shot in the knee, which threw him to the ground in great pain, with blood spurting out everywhere. Then he was hit again and I was on my own, trapped under crossfire. For the first time I felt really scared – before we had drawn on each other for strength. I sat with Andy in my arms, as his life slowly ebbed away and when I felt his body go limp, I once again said the Lord's Prayer and asked for help. I was so tired that I wished I could lie down and go to sleep, just for a short while. More and more of our troops caught up with me – we had been the advance party to recce the layout. We did manage to relay a message on the wireless set, saying 'Heavy shooting, need help' but I think that is what gave our position away.

All too soon, my rest came for ever, as I too was hit. After the initial explosion of the bullet as it tore through my body, I felt no more pain. Then, standing beside me were Claud and Andy and we three musketeers were together again, never again to be parted or targets for killing.

We came this morning and were actually with you in your dreams as you woke. You must have thought it a strange dream, but we didn't know how to talk to you in any other way. Then we were told that if we just talked to you, you would hear our story and we are so glad that we got through to you. Perhaps the time will come when you can tell our families that we are alive and well, watching over them.

I came from London, Claud from Cambridge and Andy from Sussex, all thrown together in one army, to fight shoulder to shoulder and to kill and be killed. What a strange world we lived in.

Thank you for taking down our story and for being here for us when we needed you. You are our link, our wireless message to earth from heaven.

Received July 2000.

THE FAREWELL KISS

My name is Malcolm and I was 5'9" tall and twenty-six years old when I left this world and made my way to heaven. I flew a Lancaster bomber in September 1945.

I managed to get a forty eight-hour leave and went home to Molly and my parents. I knew that something was going to happen soon, as we were getting ready for a big night raid. We all knew that the chances of coming home were rather slim.

Molly was my sweetheart and we had been courting for three years – only the war was delaying our marriage. Although I knew that all I wanted was to wed Molly, and we had planned to marry on one of my home leaves, I knew that this was not the right time. I felt, deep down, that I would never see her again.

Before that dreadful war started and tore so many lovers apart, I lived with my parents in a small town in Shropshire. It was a market town with a square. On market days it was busy with sheep and cattle, and people selling everything from flowers to pots and pans. It was a tranquil place and I loved it so much.

Before the war, I used to run kennels and breed Labradors with my parents. This is where Satin; my black Labrador comes into the story. We were inseparable and he came away with me, as the camp's mascot. Then I was on the train with my faithful companion at my feet, going home to Molly. She was a lovely girl with rosy cheeks, raven black hair and brown eyes that always shone with happiness and laughter. She was the sunshine of my soul when I was with her. We looked very much alike, and were often mistaken for brother and sister.

I was leaving the bomb-torn cities and towns behind, going deeper into the quiet countryside and then it was time to get ready. In my eagerness, I opened the carriage window and stuck my head out, to see if I could see Molly standing on the platform to welcome me. I got soot in my eye, which I knew would happen if I did something so silly. Then we were slowing down to enter the station. There she was in a pretty cotton frock, ankle socks and sandals, with a large straw hat on her head. She was holding it on with one hand and waving with the other, as the train pulled into the station.

Satin was the first off the train and I followed, carrying my kitbag. We both ran up the platform into Molly's arms. Oh, how wonderful it was to be home again. I had dreamed of this meeting and tasting her sweet kisses for weeks, since I left home for the first time. 'Oh' she cried 'I promised myself that I wouldn't cry and now look what I'm doing. I'm sorry, sweetheart.'

With Satin at our heels, we walked with our arms around each other down the long, warm lanes, where the last crops of hay were being loaded on to horse-drawn carts. Finally, we reached the front door of my parents' home and even with my eyes shut I knew the smell of my home — warm and cosy, with bramble jelly in a pan and bread in the oven. Dad was looking older and more strained, but Mum was as pretty as ever, with flour on her hands and her apron. Home, home — so full of love.

I told Dad that I had brought Satin home for good because the dangerous bombing raids were increasing and he was becoming nervous. I felt that he would be safer at home. Dad didn't have many dogs left by then, as food was harder to get. If anything happened to me, I knew Satin would be happier at home.

The moments and hours flew by, and when the subject of our wedding was brought up I said that we would wed on my next forty eight-hour leave. Somehow, I felt that I would not be able to keep that promise. I had heard many times of young brides being widowed soon after marriage, so I felt that it would be better if she remained single. If I died she would be able to get on with her life, marry and in time get over me. I wanted her, mind you, — body, mind and soul — all of her, but I kept those thoughts close to my heart.

Then, all too soon, we were on the platform waiting for the train. We were holding each other tightly and I could feel her heart beating in time with mine. I kissed and kissed her, trying to make the memory of that last farewell kiss last forever. Then I was on the train, hanging out of the window and waving goodbye until I could no longer see her. My last words were 'I love you and I'll be home.' I had said my goodbyes to Dad, Mum and Satin before I left. It was so hard to say those last words to him because I knew he understood – I could see it in his eyes. We had been friends all our lives.

As these memories fitted into the jigsaw pattern of my life's path, I settled back against the hard seat and waited for the journey to end in the Cambridge area, where I was based.

The night of the raid was wet, with threatening black clouds racing across the full moon. Our target was Berlin and, as usual, we were only told at the last minute in our final briefing, in case a careless word should be picked up by the wrong side. We took off in formation at twenty hundred hours, flying over Holland and France towards Germany. We didn't approach France in the same way on each raid, as Jerry would then have been waiting for us – we liked to keep them guessing. Searchlights lit up the sky and ack ack guns fired at us.

Flying on information supplied by the navigator, I reached the target. Berlin was a very large city. We dropped our bombs, causing a lot of damage. Black walls of bombed buildings pointed to the sky, which was lit by the raging fires. It looked like an angry furnace below.

Unfortunately, we were hit by flak from the ack ack guns as we turned for home and the damaged plane began to lose altitude. I must have been hit in the head because I felt pain there and knew that I was a 'goner'. Although I was still at the controls, I wasn't able to do anything more. My co-pilot took over, but the engine on my side was on fire and we were going down in flames.

Then I was outside my body, watching and hearing my crew screaming but unable to help them. We nose-dived into the ground, then all my crew came and stood beside me. You see, I had known I would not be going home but I wasn't scared because I accepted that my time was up.

Then I felt Satin beside me. I was sitting on a grassy bank and his head was on my lap, with so much love in those dark brown eyes. I didn't know at the time that Satin had died soon after I left him. All I knew was that he had found me and we could continue our lives together into the unknown.

Thank you for taking down my story. I'm sorry that Ginger and I came in together at the same time – we confused you with different date's etc. there are more chaps to come.

Farewell, God bless and thank you, my friend.

Received August 2000.

Dresden

My name was Ginger and I was small – about 5'1" tall – with ginger hair, of course, green eyes and lots of freckles. I was a gunner on the B17Es and my place was in the gun turret, called the nooky. It was not a job I would have chosen but I was such a small fellow and they needed a small one to get into such a place. I was actually luckier than most, as I had survived several night raids when others had been blown away by ack ack guns.

We all knew that a big raid was coming up and there were many of us going on it, not only from our airfield but others as well. It would be arranged that we should meet up with our comrades over Beachy Head at seventeen hundred hours on a February evening in 1945. I had seen pictures of Germany and Austria looking very green and a bit like England, except for the vineyards. This time we would be flying over it in the dark. Germany had lovely historical buildings, and if I had not been fighting a war I would have been following my ambition to study architecture. Now I would be taking part in a big raid which would destroy much of it.

Soon we joined forces and were flying in formation, droning on through the night. I don't know where all the planes came from but there were a lot of us – the sky seemed black with planes. Our target that night was Dresden. I had heard that the city had one of the largest zoos, so I hoped that we would not be responsible for bombing it. Raids must have been terrifying for all the animals, but I couldn't let my thoughts get in the way of our job that night.

I was so cold, like a duck stuck in an icy pond just waiting to be shot. February was bitterly cold and my hands, although in gloves, were frozen to the gun triggers.

We were retaliating for the Jerries' bombing of our beautiful cities, Coventry and London, so we had to show them that we could fight back. From the first, I had a strange feeling that I would not go home that time, but I shut it out of my mind.

Dresden lay below us and soon we were dropping bombs. God Almighty, what a noise and mess. We actually caused so much damage that when the war ended they would have to rebuild from scratch – there was nothing left.

I had fired away and then I was being blinded by smoke from somewhere. Then it happened – the plane was under fire and I was hit. Bullets tore into the nooky and cut me to pieces. I never did go home again, and I was only nineteen. I had done three 'ops' in all and the third one was my last.

Although it was just a job, there was something fascinating about hunting down and killing the enemy. Of course, we were all afraid of dying, especially of going down in flames as I couldn't get out of the nooky. There was a metal sheet, shut in by part of the floor and it was like sitting in a great glass fish bowl.

I was the fourth child in our family, the baby, and the first to die in battle. I had two older sisters – one was a nurse and the other was in the Land Army. My brother was in the navy, so we were all serving our country. Actually, there was no pain in my dying – that was the part I didn't know about and it was so peaceful. One moment I was in the thick of the action and the next I was being sucked out of it and whizzed away at speed into a very bright light.

If only someone could have told those who were afraid of death that God holds your hand and all is peaceful, with no fear at all. Everything is taken care of. I'm sorry that I came in with Malcolm but I was eager to tell you my story – then I saw that you were trying to take down two stories at the same time. I should have known that I must wait my turn.

Thanks for helping me to tell my story.

The door to the Spirit World is opening for you. God bless and thanks a lot. I don't know how Heaven coped with so many of us going over together, but we all had individual love and care.

Received August 2000.

I WAS THERE

I was an Englishman, born in Merseyside, and my name was Michael. I married in 1939 and went out to Japan the same year, as my wife was Japanese. I had met her when she went over to England on a business trip. I died in 1946 at the age of sixty-three.

We had started a new company, which did very well until the outbreak of war We were on holiday in Hiroshima when the Americans dropped the atom bomb in the August of that year.

I was there – the devastation and suffering were horrendous. I can't describe to you the wounds I saw caused by radiation burns. The animals also suffered – I saw cattle with their hides burnt off and maimed dogs and cats with terrible burns. I couldn't face the pain they were in. Then, I really wept when I saw babies dying on their mothers' backs. Yes, I could understand war and its consequences, but dropping an atom bomb on defenceless people, children and animals was beyond all possible reason. If they wanted to avenge Pearl Harbour on December 7th 1941, by attacking the Japanese, fair enough, but I couldn't understand their wiping out thousands in one blast.

Both my wife and I suffered from radiation burns. Unfortunately, my lovely little wife died in my arms, in the most dreadful agony, and I could do nothing to save her. Luckily, we had no children, so there were just the two of us to think about. Hiroshima was levelled to the ground – it had been a lovely city with temples and flowering cherry trees.

It was a lovely country, and we had been so happy there.

I died a long, slow death from cancer and the radiation burns that had eaten away at my bones and flesh, leaving me very scarred. When the end came for me I was finally at peace, and my dainty little wife was there to help me across.

Jesus said 'Suffer little children to come unto me' and so many little children did suffer before going to Him, without understanding why. I hope that nothing like that ever happens again – it was the worst possible way to die. The blast burnt all my hair off and I was nowhere near the point of the explosion. Many died slowly and there are still some survivors carrying the scars today.

Thank you for allowing me to come in to talk to you. Atomic wars must never happen again. They cause such long-term devastation to the soil, plants and all living creatures, including humans, who cannot pass on healthy genes to future generations.

Received August 2000.

ONE of our PLANES is MISSING

Hello, my name is Matthew. I was 5'4" tall, slim with black hair and brown eyes, and I was eighteen when I came over in 1941. I was an anti-aircraft gunner on a bomber and was on my first mission.

We had been on a bombing raid near Tripoli in North Africa. The Germans were pushing our front line back and we were losing ground, so bombers were required to bombard the German lines from the air. Our bombers outnumbered our tanks by four to one and were needed to defend them. It was like a tragic game – first we had them on the run and then they did the same to us.

Suddenly, we came under artillery fire from somewhere in the dunes. Our plane was hit and burst into flames, diving into the furnace of scorching sand. When the plane caught fire we scrambled to bale out, but the intense heat drove us back and only a couple got out, with their parachutes smouldering. At least they were out in the air, but we had no air to breathe, just thick, oily smoke. We were burning to death when the plane hit the ground with such force that it disintegrated.

They say that your life flashes before your eyes as you die, and mine did. I was a child again, playing football with my brothers. I think that, in the blink of an eye, you see the moments when you were happiest. Mother and Father stood clapping their hands and smiling. These were happy times in the lush green of the Gloucestershire countryside. I had pet rabbits when I was small.

Now back to the crash – oh hell, what a mess. I didn't think my life would end like that. We always felt safe in a plane while the foot soldiers took a battering. Here we were, standing around the wreckage of our plane, and most of us didn't realise that we were already dead. We stood there unburned, without a single singed hair. We saw another plane fly over, looking for us, but they couldn't see us. We were all waving and shouting, and we couldn't understand why they didn't drop us water bottles or give any other sign that we had been seen.

As the day wore on and the evening drew in fast, one or two of us decided that we were not really there at all. Then I noticed the two who had baled out with their parachutes ablaze – they walked towards us and then right through the wreckage of the plane, as though it wasn't there. The desert nights are very cold once the sun sets, such a contrast to the furnace of the day, but I felt no cold. I heard someone calling my name and I called back 'I'm here.' Others were also having their names called, so perhaps rescue had arrived after all.

What did come was not what we expected. Out of a large ball of light came some beautiful people. I didn't recognise any of them but it was so peaceful. There were also children, one of whom ran up to take my hand and pull me towards the light. 'Come on, Mister' she said, 'Come on, I'm here to take you home'. 'Home?' I asked, 'Home is in England and I'm in Africa.' 'Don't worry' she said 'I'll look after you.'

Great peace seemed to enfold us, and soon we were being transported off the earth at a great speed. I don't remember much more, until I woke up in a comfortable bed in a spotless white hospital, where nurses smiled at us and I didn't hurt any more. It felt as though I had been there for a long time, but I am now, once again, young and well with no fear of war or death. Yes, I have come home.

I can't really describe the beauty of the place I am in – I'm told it's Heaven.

There are thousands of us soldiers, sailors and airmen here, and I later found out that the ball of light is often seen by those who die on the battlefield. Angels came to take us home – a chosen number who did that rescue work. Without them we would have been lost and not known what to do. They talk us through everything and are always near to help and guide us.

The children are the sweetest I have ever known. The little girl who came to fetch me was about seven years old, and told me that her name was Jemima. She's as black as the ace of spades but what a charmer. That wee soul has been over for a long time.

Well, my friend, thank you for taking the time to sit and write down my details.

God Bless you. Matt.

BLOWN to BITS

I was twenty when I left this mortal world in 1941. My name was Josh, I was lean and 5'9" tall, with red hair, green eyes and masses of freckles. I was a South African and my family had lived in Africa for several generations. Our home was in the Orange Free State.

To die in battle is one of the most traumatic events one can go through − not like dying peaceful in one's own bed of old age. I always remember, when I was a small lad, my Grandfather saying 'I love my garden and, when I go, I would like it to be amongst my flowers. This is a bit of heaven to me.' He was lucky, because this did happen.

As for me, I was in a strange part of the country and under fire − shells had been landing fairly near to us for most of the day. We didn't stand a chance of firing back because we didn't dare raise our heads above the edge of our dugouts. The desert seemed full of flies, scorpions, spiders and snakes.

We had been pinned down by a Panzer Division near Tobruk and were trying to hold our front line against the advancing German tanks.

It was so hot, and most of us were so sunburned that we looked like natives. We were wearing khaki shorts and shirts, knee socks and boots which constantly filled with sand. Our tin hats were so hot that we only wore them under fire, as then, or when we were walking beside our tanks which we used as cover.

I had been in that bloody war for three years − three years of my young life wasted in that barren place. I had heard a rumour that thousands of our troops had been captured and were in camps, living under terrible conditions, as the Germans had no pity for them.

It felt strange that I was still in Africa, my homeland, but fighting to rid that God-forsaken place of the Germans. We hated them because they seemed to cover the land like a swarm of black flies. We thought that they were evil and uncouth, and hated what they stood for. I began to feel that I wasn't going go get out of that situation alive. My rifle was so hot and the sun was beating down on me relentlessly.

Then, I heard the rumble of tanks coming towards us. There were four of us left alive in that hole in the ground, and we were trapped like rats in a barrel, with nowhere to go. A shell blast close to our dugout took my three mates, leaving me alone. Then, just as I watched the tank tracks rising to crush me, an unexploded shell blew up in front of me. Being sucked out of my body at great speed left me standing beside the small fragments of it. My head had been blown off and my torso, arms and legs were mixed up with those of the others. What a mess. I couldn't believe that this had happened to me – not like that.

Anyway, I was out of it then, though the trauma and shock were overpowering at first. I couldn't grasp the situation, standing there alone. I thought 'How the hell can I tell my parents what has happened? Will anyone let them know?' there wasn't enough of me left to send home. The tank had caved in the sides of our dugout and we were buried under the sand, with no trace left of our ever having been there at all. The jackals would come at night and eat whatever they could find. I had seen that before, but now the idea didn't really worry me.

Once again, I could smell the orange blossoms from our groves at home. Then, Grandfather was there, looking just as I remembered him – he didn't seem to have changed at all. We embraced each other and he led me away. He had come to take me home.

Thank you for hearing my story and writing it down – the last record of my life on earth. Now I know what Grandfather meant when he said that his garden was like heaven. He was right, you know. Heaven is like a beautiful garden.

Received August 2001.

THE BATTLE of MIDWAY

My name was Simon and I was on an American battleship in the Pacific in 1942.

We were going at full steam ahead – it was a clear night, a good night for subs. It was my turn on watch and we were sailing without lights, as usual. We had had a few nights with really heavy seas and, oh boy, when the waves are high in the Pacific they are mighty high. With the heavy seas, visibility was bad, so when we had calm nights we were apt to relax a bit too much – for one thing, we weren't so seasick.

Then something caught my eye, glinting in the moonlight. It was the top of a periscope – oh God, a sub. At this moment we also picked it up on radar, at five hundred yards and closing. Then, like silver darts dashing through the water, came torpedoes, first one and then another. With a blinding flash and an explosion we were hit amidships. I was thrown off my feet, landing heavily some yards away, winded. I was sure that my arm was broken and I ached all over, but there was no time to think of myself.

There was blind panic on board and I heard the call of 'Abandon Ship.' We were sinking and those words meant everyone for himself. I jumped off the ship and it seemed an endless moment, when time, life and the universe all stood still. Then I hit the sea, and sailors were falling on top of each other. There were screams, smoke and oil catching fire on the surface of the sea – pure hell all around us, with not enough lifeboats.

Then the sub came out of the water and stood some five hundred yards from us, as though assessing the damage they had done. I don't know how long I was in the water – at first we would call to each other, trying to keep in contact with another human voice, as it was so important not to feel alone. Fewer and fewer seemed to be around me, while I was hanging on to a piece of debris. Then I don't remember any more, so my time was up. Then I was over here and not alone any more, as all my mates were also here.

I wanted to come, as I know quite a few other chaps have come through to you to tell you their stories. There were thousands of us who went missing, were presumed dead and no trace of us was ever found. War must be stopped. On Armistice Day, the world remembers the dead, but who remembers us? There were no dog tags, and no mention of where or when we were killed. You could almost say that we were ghost airmen, soldiers and sailors. It was such a waste of young men and women, the cream of the nation, and there was so much heartbreak for those left behind. It must STOP.

I was just seventeen when I caught it. God bless and thank you for listening to me.

Pa said I was wasted in the Navy, and that I should have been a politician.

Simon was a thin youth, 5'6" tall with a slight frame. He looked older than he was, so he was under age when he joined up with his brother. He had red hair and green eyes.
Received on Remembrance Day in 1996.

THE LAST JUMP

My name was James and I was only eighteen, serving the second year of my National Service in 1951. I was of medium build, with grey eyes and mousy hair, and my home was in Somerset. We were all National Servicemen, straight out from camp to Korea, and were jokingly called 'The virgin soldiers.' We were facing our first jump and none of us had ever killed someone else.

There I was, sitting on a small seat with my back against the metal interior of the fuselage, shoulder to shoulder with two others and wearing my battle dress and a parachute. We were being given last minute instructions, but most of the words were drowned out by the noise of the plane. All twenty-four of us were going to be dropped over rough terrain, including jungle and swamps. Our unit was to reinforce the troops who were already there, as they had encountered heavy resistance from the Chinese. In Korea there isn't much open ground for safe parachuting, so our fate lay in the hands of the pilot and God.

I was quite excited but also scared. Our worst fears were either to be shot in the air, or to land in the trees. We had so much gear to carry that we needed an extra free hand to pull the cord. I was sure that I had missed important details of our briefing, so I prayed for a safe landing and took a deep breath as we stood up. Our cords were clipped to the guiding wire above our heads. I put my hand on the shoulder of the young soldier in front of me and whispered 'Good luck and a safe landing. I'll see you when we get down.'

The red light came on, went out and all too soon the green light came on, and we were moving forward ready to jump. Then I felt a strong hand on my back and the command 'Jump.' I shut my eyes and stepped out into nothing, dropping like a stone and trying to catch my breath. The wind pressed against my face, sucking the first gasps of air out of my lungs. Then the parachute opened and I was yanked upwards at the rate of knots. Then all went quiet and, looking down between my feet, I saw a blur of green jungle.

The wind was pulling me off course, and for a moment I panicked as the treetops loomed towards me, getting closer every second. Then, I felt a strong hand grab me and pull me free of the trees. I glanced around in gratitude but could see no one. I felt a strong presence – perhaps God had stretched out his hand to help me in my hour of need. I thought of the St. Christopher medallion round my neck and said 'Thank you.' Then I was coming down near the river – neither the first nor the last to come down. I tried throwing myself from side to side, to persuade the parachute to move away from the river. As this was my first real jump, I couldn't remember what else to do in those circumstances.

Then I hit a tree and my parachute collapsed around me. I heard a shout 'Oh God, he's hit the only bloody tree in this spot.' I started falling through the branches, thinking that I must stop soon, when there was a sharp pain in my neck and it was all over for me. I must have broken my neck. Then, I was standing with my mates at the bottom of the tree, looking up at my limp body – it was just hanging there, swaying to and fro. 'Come on, guys, cut me down' I called to the boys, but no one heard me. Instead, they all walked away, so I followed. I kept looking back at my body hanging there, and decided to go back to the tree and wait for help.

Help came, but not in the way I had expected it. An old man and two small boys walked by, and one child pointed and called out. The old man put his finger to his lips, anxious that they should not be heard. The older child climbed up the tree, took out a knife and started to cut the straps of my parachute, releasing my body which slumped to the ground. He then proceeded to tear the parachute out of the tree. The old man scraped at the soft earth beneath the tree with his bare hands, making a shallow grave into which he rolled my body. He covered it with earth, branches and grass to conceal it. I just stood there and watched. With the silk down, they hurriedly left the spot and returned to their village.

Then, I quite clearly heard a beautiful voice saying 'Come on, we must go. You can't stay here any more – your work here is ended and it's time to go home'. Then I was sucked up from the ground and felt as though I was flying at tremendous speed towards a bright, warm light. The voice was with me all the time and then I was home, where I have been for a long time now.

Thank you for listening to my story.

Received 24th March 2000.